MEN-AT-ARMS SERIES

EDITOR: MARTIN WIND

German Military Police Units

1939-45

Text by GORDON WILLIAMSON

Colour plates by RON VOLSTAD

OSPREY PUBLISHING LONDON

Published in 1989 by
Osprey Publishing Ltd
59 Grosvenor Street, London W1X 9DA
© Copyright 1989 Osprey Publishing Ltd

British Library Cataloguing in Publication Data
Williamson, Gordon
    German military police units, 1939–1945.—(Men-at-arms, 211).
    1. Germany. Heer, 1933–1945
    I. Title   II. Series
    355´.00943

    ISBN 0-85045-902-8

Filmset in Great Britain
Printed through Bookbuilders Ltd, Hong Kong

Acknowledgements

I have been fortunate in my research to make contact with two veterans of the Feldgendarmerie of the famed 'Hermann Göring' Fallschirmpanzer-korps, who provided several rare photographs, including shots of the Luftwaffe-pattern Feldgendarmerie gorget being worn. To these gentlemen, Herren Herbert E. Kail and Wolfgang Dinger, I am most grateful. My thanks also to former Feldgendarmen Heinz Heuer and Hans Hauser for photographic and documentary material. Thanks are also due to Munin Verlag of Osnabrück for permission to reproduce photographs from their archives; and to Brian L. Davis, Fred Stephens and Josef Charita for photographic contributions. Readers interested in further study of the history of the German Military Police through the ages are referred to the excellent work by Karl-Heinz Böckle, *Feldgendarmen, Feldjäger Militärpolizisten*, published by Motorbuch Verlag.

Artist's Note
Readers may care to note that the original paintings from which the colour plates in this book were prepared are available for private sale. All reproduction copyright whatsoever is retained by the publisher. All enquiries should be addressed to:

Ronald B. Volstad
P.O. Box 2730
Canmore, Alberta,
Canada ToL oMo

The publishers regret that they can enter into no correspondence upon this matter.

Introduction

The military policeman must be one of the least appreciated (certainly by his fellow soldiers) yet most indispensable military figures in modern history. In the mobile warfare of the 20th century no army could keep its vital supply convoys on the move and its supply routes open without the military policeman. If his fellow soldiers' opinion of him is usually expressed in expletives, then those in higher command with a good overall view, certainly valued his service—witness some of the views expressed through the ages by field commanders about their MPs:

'*You cannot have a good army without a police force within*' (Napoleon Bonaparte).

'*The Field Marshall Commander in Chief expresses his satisfaction with the work of the Military Police. . . . The orderliness which has prevailed behind the front is directly attributed to their efficiency and devotion*' (The Adjutant General, British Expeditionary Force, 1918).

'*The Battle of Normandy and subsequent battles would never have been won but for the work and co-operation of Provost on the traffic routes*' (Field Marshal B. L. Montgomery, 1945).

'*The Feldjäger have fulfilled their psychological purpose. Their actions have rapidly gained them a reputation . . . their help and support were much sought after*' (General der Flieger Speidel, 1948).

The British Corps of Royal Military Police can trace its roots back tenuously as far as the Earl Marshals of Norman times; and Germany's Feldjägerkorps likewise has a long and distinguished tradition stretching back to the 'Profoss' of the 16th century. In 1740 Friedrich II established the *Feldjägerkorps zu Pferd* which shortly afterwards had its title amended to *Reitendes Feldjägerkorps*. From these troops were drawn men for the following duties: *Kolonnenjäger*—to control and protect traffic routes; *Kurierjäger*—to carry impor-

A typical Army Feldgendarmerie NCO on traffic control duty. Well wrapped up against the winter cold, he wears the motorcyclist's waterproof overcoat and heavy gloves. On his standard Army issue belt he carries a 9mm Walther P38 pistol in a black leather holster. A woollen toque is worn to protect the ears and neck. The ubiquitous gorget and traffic wand indicate his status as a Military Policeman. (B. L. Davis)

tant messages and orders; *Furierjäger*—to accompany and protect members of the Royal Family. Shortly after the founding of the *Feldjägerkorps zu Pferd*, the *Feldjägerkorps zu Fuss* was formed in 1741.

The Feldjägerkorps served with distinction during the Napoleonic Wars, and the Franco-Prussian War of 1870. Alongside the Feldjägerkorps, the *Gendarmerie* or civil police was to develop a military branch of *Feldgendarmerie*, which grew to overtake the Feldjägerkorps as Germany's principal provost arm.

On the outbreak of war in 1914 the German armies had at their disposal 33 Feldgendarmerie Troops, each of around 60 NCOs and men. Like its British counterpart at that time, the Feldgendarmerie was officered by personnel on a temporary attachment from other arms, mostly Cavalry. The standard Feldgendarmerie patrol consisted of a sergeant (*Obergendarm*) and two junior NCOs (*Unteroffiziere* or *Gefreite*). In addition, temporary Field Police or *Hilfsgendarmen* were employed. By

the end of the Great War a total of 115 Feldgendarmerie units had been formed, and additionally a Feldgendarmeriekorps of five cavalry squadrons for special missions, which ultimately reached regimental strength before the war's end. The conclusion of the Great War saw the disbandment of the Feldjägerkorps and the Feldgendarmerie. During the period from 1919 to 1939, no military police formations existed in the German army, though army street patrols policed garrison areas.

If the overlap of functions between the Feldjägerkorps and Feldgendarmerie in the Great War seems confusing, the multiplicity of police formations used by the German war machine during the Second World War seems astonishing. Among the many existing police units were the Feldgendarmerie, Feldjägerkorps, Geheime Feld Polizei Heeresstreifendienst, Zugwache, Bahnhofswache Marinekusten-Polizei, and numerous Polize Schutzen Regimenter. This is without including the numerous state security organs, such as the

An Army Feldgendarmerie junior NCO on traffic duty on the Eastern Front in 1942. Note once again the waterproof coat, gorget and traffic wand. The Horch field car is typical of the type of light vehicle used by Feldgendarmerie personnel. It is finished in a tan colour with green and reddish-brown mottled camouflage. (J. Charita)

In this unusual scene an Oberfeldwebel of Army Feldgendarmerie uses an NSU Kettenkrad half-tracked motorcycle to pull a light truck through the mire of a Russian road in the spring thaw. The Oberfeldwebel wears the M1938 pattern Feldmütze. The Kettenkrad was not standard issue to Feldgendarmerie units. (J. Charita)

Sicherheitsdienst which were also to be found in combat areas.

Much hated by their fellow soldiers, the German military policemen were known by more sinister nicknames than their British counterparts, the Redcaps': 'Chained Dogs' and 'Headhunters' were just two of the epithets commonly used.

At the end of the Second World War, the skills of the German Military Police were quickly appreciated by the British and Americans, who used several entire companies of fully armed Feldgendarmen and Feldjäger as auxiliaries to assist their own hard-pressed police formations. In the chaotic conditions of the immediate post-war period the experienced manpower provided by these troops was of great help to the occupying authorities.

When the German Army was re-formed in 1955 one of the first units to be established was a Military Police Company. In 1956 these *Militär Polizei* were granted the use of the traditional title 'Feldjäger'. The Bundeswehr today fields Feldjäger units in each military district (*Wehrbereich*) which in the case of mobilisation would be strengthened by reservists. There are no Air Force or Naval Provost units, the Feldjäger having authority over all three services.

The traditional gorget and cuffband are no longer used as identifying symbols. Instead, more in keeping with other NATO countries, a distinctive white belt and pistol holster are worn; a white armband bearing the legend *Feldjäger* is also used on duty. The traditional Military Police branch-of-service colour of orange-red has been retained as piping to the shoulder straps and underlay for the collar patches. The beret used for everyday duties is in the same red colour as that used by the British RMP; the badge worn thereon bears the traditional emblem of the Feldjäger, the Guards Star and motto '*Suum Cuique*', reinforcing the traditional links with the Feldjäger of Imperial times.

Although countless books have been written on the subject of the armed forces of the Third Reich, little has appeared on the subject of the Military Police forces. This is despite the fact that there is a great demand for original examples of Military Police memorabilia among collectors. It is hoped that this book will go some way towards filling that gap.

Feldgendarmerie des Heeres

The Feldgendarmerie was formed on the mobilisation of the German Army in 1939. Its members were, in the main, experienced former civil policemen from the civil Gendarmerie (particularly the Motorisierte Gendarmerie) and serving Army NCOs. The command structure of the Feldgendarmerie began at the Oberkommando des Heeres or OKH (High Command of the Army) where the senior ranking officer of the Feldgendarmerie would be attached. He was under the direct control of the Quartermaster-General of the German Armies and was responsible for all matters relating to the Feldgendarmerie including personnel administration, postings, etc. He was also responsible for allocation of tasks to the Feldgendarmerie and monitoring its performance, for laying down traffic regulations, and standardising Feldgendarmerie training procedures.

The next level of command lay with each Armee Oberkommando, to which was attached a Feldgendarmerie staff officer responsible for Feldgendarmerie matters within the area of that army. The staff officer controlled all the Feldgendarmerie units attached to that Army and was responsible for maintaining order and discipline, and especially for traffic control and route maintenance during large-scale troop movements.

Each Field Army of the Wehrmacht had under its command a Feldgendarmerie Bataillon and each Division a Feldgendarmerietrupp.

A typical Feldgendarmerie Bataillon of the Second World War would have the following structure:

Command Group: one officer, one warrant officer, two NCOs, three Other Ranks. *Vehicles*: one field car, one small bus.

M T Section: one NCO, three Other Ranks. *Vehicles*: one motorcycle, one field car.

Platoons (× 3): one officer, three NCO drivers, 17 NCOs, ten Other Ranks. *Vehicles*: three motorcyles, two motorcycle combinations, eight Kubelwagens.

Support Group: one each NCO clerk, M T NCO, armourer NCO, cook NCO, cook OR, armourer OR, clerk OR, cobbler; and four driver ORs. *Vehicles*: two × 2-ton vehicles, two × 3-ton vehicles.

A typical Feldgendarmerietrupp in an Army Division (in this case Armoured) would be as follows: one officer commanding, two officer platoon commanders, three NCO motorcycle drivers, three OR motorcycle drivers, eight NCO drivers, four OR drivers, 13 OR drivers and 30 NCOs. Vehicle allocation to a typical Feldgendarmerietrupp in an Armoured or Motorised Division would comprise: six solo motorcycles; four motorcycle combinations (sidecar with an MG34 or MG42 machine gun); 17 light field cars (usually the VW 'Kubelwagen'); two × 2-ton vehicles (generally a heavy field car such as a 4 × 4 Horch or

Hauptmann Hans Hauser as Chef der Feldgendarmerietrupp 498 during an inspection trip in Sicily 1942. Note that on the tropical field dress worn on this occasion only the shoulder strap Waffenfarbe indicates his Feldgendarmerie status; no sleeve eagle or cuffband are worn. From photographic evidence it would appear that the use of full Feldgendarmerie sleeve insignia on the tropical dress was very rare. Hauser later won the Knight's Cross on 6 May 1945 when serving in SS-Panzer-Grenadier-Regiment 4 'Der Führer' with the 'Das Reich' Division. (Hans Hauser)

Steyr; and two × 3-ton vehicles (usually an Opel Blitz or similar light truck).

Personal armament of the Feldgendarmerie was initially restricted to light weapons. A wide range of automatic pistols was used, NCOs and men normally carrying a Walther P38 or a Luger PO8, whereas officers often favoured the more compact Walther PP or PPK. Most NCOs carried the MP38/40 machine pistol, and while the Mauser Kar98k rifle can be seen in wartime photos of Feldgendarmerie personnel, it was not widely used. The superb MG34 or MG42 belt-fed machine guns were also used by Feldgendarmerie units as a vehicle weapon or for defending road blocks. As the war drew towards its end, many Feldgendarmerie personnel found themselves thrown into front-line combat, and the deadly Panzerfaust anti-tank projectile saw frequent use (see the report of Heinz Heuer's success against Soviet tanks in the battle for Berlin).

Former policemen drafted into the Feldgendarmerie were allocated military ranks in keeping with their former police status as follows:

Wachtmeister.....................*Unteroffizier der Feldgendarmerie*
Oberwachtmeister..............*Feldwebel der Feldgendarmerie*
Bezirkswachtmeister ....*Oberfeldwebel der Feldgendarmerie*
Hauptwachtmeister ....*Stabsfeldwebel der Feldgendarmerie*
Meister/Obermeister...........*Leutnant der Feldgendarmerie*
Inspektor ....*Oberleutnant der Feldgendarmerie*

The Feldgendarmerie, in military terms, had similar responsibilities to the *Ordnungspolizei* in civilian life. Amongst the many and varied tasks of the Feldgendarmerie were the following (by no means a complete list):

Traffic control; maintaining military order and discipline; collection and escorting of prisoners of war; collection and redirection of stragglers; prevention of looting; supervision and control of civilian populace in occupied areas; disarming civilians; checking captured enemy soldiers for documents, maps or other useful information; checking papers of soldiers in transit or on leave; collection of fallen enemy propaganda leaflets and prevention of distribution of such material; searching for shot-down enemy fliers; providing street patrols in occupied areas; prevention of sabotage; control of evacuees during retreats; duties of a security nature in co-operation with the *Geheime Feldpolizei* (i.e. counter-espionage, monitoring

A standard model 1936 Feldbluse of an Army Feldgendarmerie Oberfeldwebel. All the insignia are machine-stitched to the tunic with the exception of the shoulder straps which are removable.

politically suspect persons, etc); apprehending deserters; border control; anti-partisan duties. After the occupation of Czechoslovakia and Poland, Feldgendarmerie training schools were set up in Prague and in Litzmannstadt-Görnau.

The Feldgendarmerie's authority allowed them to pass through secured areas, roadblocks, guard posts, etc, and to conduct searches of both personnel and property wherever deemed necessary, and in doing so they could commandeer assistance from any other military personnel. In the event of dispute, any Feldgendarme held superiority over any other soldier of similar rank from any other branch of the services. Although, like military policemen of any nation, the Feldgendarmerie were best remembered by the common soldier as strict disciplinarians, ever ready to pounce on an 'innocent' squaddie, there is no doubt that their greatest contribution to the war effort was the

A close-up of the Feldgendarmerie gorget and sleeve eagle; note the well-detailed stitching of the latter. Many original examples of the Feldgendarmerie gorget still have the luminosity on the painted details even after 40 years or more. (B. L. Davis)

control and security of supply routes to the front line. In this respect the Feldgendarme was no different to the MP of any other nation; no army can function without secured supply routes and efficient traffic control.

Towards the end of the war, many Feldgendarmen found themselves used as front line combat troops in desperate defensive or counter-attack movements, particularly on the Eastern Front. Several Feldgendarmen were decorated for gallantry during these hectic days. The following soldiers were awarded the German Cross in Gold: Maj. Werner Weber (Feldgendarmerie Abteilung 682): Leutnant der Reserve Peter Scholz (Feldgendarmerietrupp 1544): Obergefreiter Hans Schlotter (Bahnhofswacheabteilung 2); and Oberleutnant der Reserve Johannes Kandziora (2/Feldgendarmerie Abt. 531).

The most highly decorated of all serving Feldgendarmen was Leutnant der Feldgendarmerie Heinz Heuer, decorated for his heroism during the battle for Berlin in 1945; Heinz Heuer was the only Feldgendarme to be decorated with the coveted Knight's Cross of the Iron Cross. (Former Feldgendarmerie officer Hans Hauser was also awarded the Knight's Cross, but at the time of the award was serving as an SS-Sturmbannführer with a Waffen-SS Panzer Grenadier Regiment.)

According to Herr Heuer, in these late days of the war Feldgendarmerie personnel caught by the Soviets could expect short shrift; indeed, rumours abounded of a 'bounty' offered for the head of any Feldgendarme taken. Certainly these rumours were taken seriously by the Germans; each Feldgendarme was issued with a second *Soldbuch* (ID or 'pay book') falsely showing the holder as an 'ordinary' soldier whose capture would be uninteresting to the Soviets. When capture was imminent the Feldgendarme would merely throw away his duty gorget and real *Soldbuch* and on capture present his fake *Soldbuch* in the hope of avoiding execution. This makes the tale of Heuer's actions in the last few days of the war, and his eventual capture even more impressive.

Leutnant der Feldgendarmerie Heinz Heuer

Heinz Heuer was born in Berlin on 2 August 1918. He began his military service at the age of 18, joining 5/Flak Regiment 12 in Döberitz and subsequently 10/Flak Regiment 32 in Berlin. On 1 November 1938 he joined the Police and attended several Police Training Schools before joining the Technical Police School in Berlin to complete his instruction. Assigned to the Ordnungspolizei HQ, he was subsequently attached 'z.b.V.' (for special duties) to the Foreign Office and to the OKW/Abwehr foreign department. During the war Heuer served on all fronts and saw action with the famous 'Brandenburgers'.

1945 saw Heuer as a highly experienced Oberfeldwebel der Feldgendarmerie leading a small Kampfgruppe in the defence of Berlin. Heuer and his group were called before Gen. Krebs on 16 April 1945 and given a special task. A suspected Russian command post in a certain area was to be 'cleared out', and Heuer, with a small band of around 28 men, was to do the job. When searching for the enemy post, Heuer and his men encountered an enemy tank unit around 40 strong. On the night of 21 April, Heuer and his men surprised and overcame the guards on the Russian command post and captured many maps and important documents. On his return Heuer and his men came upon others from their group in action against the enemy tanks spotted earlier. They joined the action; and of the 27 enemy tanks destroyed, Heuer's personal score came to an amazing 13, achieved using the

'Panzerfaust' hand-held anti-tank projectile. On his successful return Heuer reported to Gen. Krebs and informed him of his unit's achievements. Krebs was delighted with the captured Soviet material and Heuer's destruction of so many enemy tanks; and in the presence of Gens. Krebs, Burgdorf and Fegelein, Heuer was decorated with the Knight's Cross. He was also given a field promotion to Leutnant der Feldgendarmerie.

Following the success of his mission, Heuer was given a further special task: to take a personal

Hauptfeldwebel Heinz Heuer, the sole serving Feldgendarmerie recipient of the Knights Cross of the Iron Cross. In this photograph taken prior to his award-winning actions, Heuer wears the standard M1936 pattern Army Feldbluse; note that at this late stage of the war, no arm eagle or cuffband are worn, only the orange piping indicating Heuer's status as a Feldgendarme. Note the whistle lanyard on the right shoulder, and the Driver's Badge in gold on the left sleeve. (Heinz Heuer)

message from Hitler to SS-Gen. Felix Steiner. Heuer set off by motorcycle, but was captured by Soviet troops. In the style of the best spy stories, Heuer managed to chew up and swallow the message before the Soviets could stop him. The Soviets were in no mood to take prisoners and Heuer, together with some other captured Germans, was given a spade and told to dig himself a shallow grave. Execution was to be immediate. Having completed this most macabre of tasks, the doomed Germans were allowed a last cigarette. In the next few minutes an artillery barrage came crashing in, forcing the Soviet guards to take cover, and Heuer and his comrades made good their escape. However, as the war ended shortly afterwards, Heuer soon found himself in Soviet captivity again. He was held first in Tscheljabinsk in Siberia, and then at a punishment camp in Oms. With the help of a Russian woman doctor, Heuer was able to arrange repatriation to Berlin; once there, however, he was denounced to the GPU and arrested once again. Severely debilitated after his captivity, Heuer now weighed a mere six stone (about 85lb). Luckily, with the connivance of a sympathetic Russian officer, Heuer managed to escape once again and made his way to the Western Zone.

Heuer's military decorations included the Iron Cross 2nd and 1st Class, Wound Badge in Silver, East Front Campaign Medal, War Merit Cross 2nd Class with Swords, Driver's Badge in Gold, two Gold and three Silver Tank Destruction Awards and the Knight's Cross. After the war Heuer returned to a police career. He was still alive at the time of writing.

Uniforms and Insignia
The special identifying insignia worn by the Feldgendarmerie were as follows:
Headgear: Orange-red *Waffenfarbe* was worn by Feldgendarmerie troops as piping to the crown and cap band of the Schirmmütze or peaked cap and as an inverted chevron of braid over the cockade on the side cap and soft peaked tropical Einheitsfeldmütze. *Uniform*: The orange-red Waffenfarbe was also used as piping to the centre of the collar patch bars, to the shoulder straps for NCOs and other ranks, and as underlay to officers' shoulder straps. In addition to the Waffenfarbe, the

A peaked cap—Schirmmütze—of an Army Feldgendarmerie officer. Piping to the crown and cap band is in orange-red Waffenfarbe. NCOs' versions were identical but for the use of a black patent leather chinstrap retained by two black buttons in place of the officer's silver chin cords.

Feldgendarme was identified by the Polizei-pattern upper left sleeve eagle. This consisted of a machine-embroidered spread eagle and swastika within a wreath of oakleaves. The swastika was executed in black thread, the rest of the insignia in orange-red for other ranks and in silver thread for officers. On the lower left sleeve was worn a cuffband bearing the legend 'Feldgendarmerie' in Gothic script. The band was woven in brown artificial silk with grey woven edging and lettering. Variants exist in grey machine embroidery on brown felt, with no edging (this type is commonly reproduced, but with braid edging); and a rare specimen is known on a field grey backing.

Troops from other branches of service on temporary attachment to the Feldgendarmerie wore a special armband in green cloth with the legend 'Feld/Gendarmerie' in two lines of orange script. Both woven and embroidered versions are known.

Probably the best known of all identifying features of the Feldgendarme was the duty gorget or *Ringkragen*. This was a half-moon shaped thin sheet metal stamping with a raised edge for strength. It was finished in a silver-grey colour and featured at each tip a standard stippled-finish button painted in luminous yellow-green. In the centre was a large spread eagle and swastika, also in luminous finish, over a dark grey scroll bearing the legend 'Feldgendarmerie' in luminous Latin script letters. The reverse of the gorget was usually covered with field grey cloth or card, and had a flat 'tongue' in the centre which was slipped into the tunic buttonhole to prevent the gorget from swinging about. The gorget was suspended by a neck chain of plain flat links.

Above The standard Army-pattern 'Feldgendarmerie' cuffband, machine-woven in the so-called 'Bevo' style in brown artificial silk with grey edges and lettering. The reverse of the cuffband is a mass of grey threads, rather than the 'chequerboard' effect normally found on most SS-type Bevo cuffbands.

Below Rarer, though less sought after by collectors, is this machine-embroidered pattern. The grey thread letters are embroidered on a brown felt band. This type is commonly reproduced, but usually with silver braid edging.

An Army Feldgendarme walks through the shattered streets : Brussels in May 1944. Although rather faded, the original early shows the Arm eagle and 'Feldgendarmerie' cuffband being worn. The lack of NCO Tresse on the tunic collar implies that this is a private soldier. He is armed only with an automatic pistol. (J. Charita)

parachute landings; checking soldiers' leave papers in the search for deserters; and supporting local *Volkssturm* units.

Elements of Feldjägerkommando III were the last German troops to lay down their arms after the Second World War. When troops in the south of Germany surrendered to the Americans, the US forces realised that with huge numbers of German personnel surrendered or attempting to surrender, the Feldjäger could be of great use in maintaining order. The *Oberbefehlshaber Süd*, Generalfeldmarschall Kesselring, agreed to put his Feldjäger at the disposal of the US Army; and for several weeks after the cease-fire the Feldjäger—fully armed and equipped—remained on duty. Their tasks included overseeing German adherence to the cease-fire; maintaining order among German troops; maintaining order in occupied areas; controlling traffic; and collecting individual stragglers. Feldjägerkommando III finally laid down its arms as late as 23 June 1946.

The Feldgendarmerie and Feldjäger were the principal provost units of the German Army in the Second World War. A number of other lesser units also provided provost support, and these are briefly described in the following sections.

The exceptionally rare warrant disc of the Geheime Feld Polizei. Note the circular rather than oval shape, and the use of Army rather than State-pattern eagle and swastika on the obverse. (Peter Groch)

Uniforms and Insignia

No special tunic insignia in the form of distinctive Waffenfarbe, sleeve eagles, cuffbands, etc., were introduced. The Feldjäger wore normal white infantry Waffenfarbe piping. A special shoulder cypher in the form of a monogram 'Fj' in Latin script was produced, but it is unknown to what extent, if any, this was ever worn. A red cloth duty armband was worn bearing the legend *Oberkommando der Wehrmacht/Feldjäger* in two lines of black Latin script. Photographic evidence seems to indicate that although this took the form of an armband or brassard, it was worn on the lower left sleeve in the position in which a cuffband would normally be worn. The principal identifying insignia of the Feldjäger was, as for his Feldgendarmerie counterpart, the gorget. The Feldjäger gorget was identical in appearance and design to that for the Feldgendarmerie, the only difference being in the scroll legend reading *Feldjägerkorps*.

Geheime Feldpolizei

The Geheime Feldpolizei—GeFePo or GFP—were Germany's 'plain clothes' military police, somewhat similar to the British Special Investigation Branch (SIB) of the Military Police. It was formed in 21 July 1939 by order of the chief of the

The Polizei-style sleeve eagle and woven Feldgendarmerie cuffband were withdrawn from wear in 1944. This may have been for economy, but it seems likely to have been for security reasons. As previously mentioned, Feldgendarmen were issued with two Soldbuchs to help disguise their identity when captured. Whereas the true Soldbuch could be easily discarded, machine-stitched insignia could not be so easily removed in a hurry. As it seems that only Feldgendarmerie troops were specifically instructed to remove the special identifying insignia, security would appear to have been a prime factor.

Feldjägerkorps

By 1943 Germany's fortunes were on the turn. Military reverses were common on all fronts; and, naturally enough, the morale of the German soldier, for so long used to easy victories, began to drop. Many able-bodied men made every effort possible to avoid service at the front line, especially in Russia. All measures taken to arrest the decline in morale fell well short of target. Strong measures were called for; and in November 1943 an entirely new force was created—the Feldjägerkorps. Although it carried the traditional title of the Feldjäger of the Imperial Army, its functions and authority were far removed from those of its Imperial forebears. These men were to be no ordinary military policemen.

All men taken into the Feldjäger had at least three years' front line combat service and had won at least the Iron Cross 2nd Class. Their ranking officers were also required to have had considerable experience at senior command levels. These men would know how the common soldier 'at the sharp end' felt; and would thus have the moral stature for their difficult work. These were military men, hardened by experience, who would brook no political interference with their duties.

The Feldjägerkorps consisted of three Feldjäger-kommandos: Feldjägerkommando I, formed in Königsberg, was commanded by Gen. der Flieger Ernst Müller. Feldjägerkommando II, formed in Breslau, was commanded by Gen. der Panzertruppe Kempf, Gen. der Infanterie von Oven and Gen. Moser. Feldjägerkommando III, formed in Vienna, was commanded by Gen. der Infanterie von Scheele, Gen. der Infanterie Grase, and ultimately by Gen. der Flieger Speidel.

The basic Feldjäger unit was the patrol or 'Streife' comprising an officer and three experienced NCOs. Each Feldjägerabteilung had approximately 50 such patrols, formed into three companies. Five such Feldjägerabteilungen comprised a Feldjäger-Regiment; and each Feldjägerkommando had one such Regiment under its control.

The Feldjägerkorps was answerable only to the Oberkommando der Wehrmacht, and thus its authority was great. The commanding officer of a Feldjägerkommando had equal status to an Army Commander, with the authority to execute punishment on all Wehrmacht—and Waffen-SS—personnel. Although his disciplinary authority was great the Feldjäger could not interfere with military decisions. In case of dispute the Feldjäger were fully entitled to settle any arguments at gunpoint.

Both Feldjägerkommando I and II saw out the war on the Eastern Front, so records of their activities are extremely sparse. Feldjägerkommando III ended the war in the West, however, and its commander, Gen. der Flieger Speidel, survived.

The Feldjäger operated approximately 12 miles behind, and parallel to, the front line. Their function was to preserve order and discipline, prevent panic retreats, and act as a 'safety net'. Patrols on all routes leading back from the front (including rivers etc) collected stragglers and other superfluous manpower and sent them back to stiffen the front line. Scattered elements of units which had taken a hammering at the front, and individual stragglers, were often assembled at collection points into 'ad hoc' units. At the same time deserters were apprehended and dealt with, and escaped enemy POWs rounded up. With their immense powers, Feldjäger would think nothing of rounding up the hated party functionaries or 'Golden Pheasants' and sending them to the front.

Working in close co-operation with local Army Commanders, the duties of the Feldjäger could also include: traffic control, including reconnoitring and marking of harbour areas; arranging removal of bomb debris, etc, to keep routes open; assembling quick-reaction units (including commandeering civil vehicles where necessary) in the case of enemy

Oberkommando der Wehrmacht, Generaloberst Wilhelm Keitel. Members of the GFP were classed as *Wehrmachtsbeamten* or 'military officials'.

The Geheime Feldpolizei was commanded by a *Heerespolizeichef* or Chief of Army Police, who was attached directly to the Oberkommando des Heeres; initially this post held a rank equivalent to the military rank of major. Subordinate to the Heeresfeldpolizeichef but also carrying a status equal to major was the *Feldpolizeidirektor*. This official reported to Armee Oberkommando level and controlled a Geheime Feldpolizei *Gruppe*. There were no 'other rank' grades in the Geheime Feldpolizei as initially formed; Any non-commissioned personnel required were drawn from available troops commandeered as '*Hilfs-Feldpolizeibeamten*' or 'auxiliary field police officials'. The rank grading for Heeresfeldpolizeichef was upgraded to the equivalent of *Oberst* (colonel) on 24 July 1939. The structure was once again reformed after the Luftwaffe gained its own Geheime Feldpolizei in 1943. The new structure of ranks was as follows:

Feldpolizeichef der Wehrmacht.......*Generalmajor* equivalent
Heeresfeldpolizeichef.....................*Oberst*
Oberfeldpolizeidirektor   *Oberstleutnant*
Feldpolizeidirektor   *Major*
Feldpolizeikommissar ....*Hauptmann*
Feldpolizeiobersekretär/inspektor .....*Oberleutnant*
Feldpolizeisekretär ....*Leutnant*
Feldpolizeiassistant........................All NCOs

The functions of the Geheime Feldpolizei were many, and included counter-espionage, counter-sabotage, detection of treasonable activity and counter-propaganda. The Geheime Feldpolizei also assisted the Army legal system in investigations for courts martial.

Officials of the Geheime Feldpolizei, largely recruited from the Criminal Police, had similar authority to those of the Polizei and Sicherheitsdienst. In carrying out their duties they could wear whatever civilian clothes or uniform was considered appropriate. Each member had, in addition to his ID disc and *Soldbuch*, a pass in green card showing his photo in civil and military dress, and a police warrant disc.

By virtue of his special identity papers, the GFP official was entitled to pass through militar roadblocks; enter military buildings; utilise militar signals and communications equipment; com mandeer military vehicles; procure military sup plies and accommodation wherever necessary in th execution of his duty; and use public transpor systems free. Some of the general tasks allocated t the GFP official could include: personal escort t various military VIPs; assistance to state securit personnel in counter-espionage work; interrogatio of captured enemy soldiers; detection of enem

A shoulder strap for a Hauptfeldwebel of Army Feldgendar merie attached to the Geheime Feldpolizei; the cypher is i silvered metal. Personnel on temporary attachment to th GFP wore only the cypher pinned to their normal shoulde straps.

aliens using German ID/uniforms, etc.; securing of telegram and mail facilities on entering enemy territory; securing of railway terminals; searching out enemy radio equipment and signal detection; rounding-up inflammatory and libellous materials; precautionary measures against rail sabotage; detection of enemy agents dropped by parachute; assistance at customs posts against smuggling; watch on river traffic; prevention of unauthorised travel; checking travel papers; watch on neutral personnel (i.e. diplomatic and military attachés, etc.) and on foreign newspaper correspondents, etc.

The overlap between some of the duties of the Feldgendarmerie and Geheime Feldpolizei is clear but by no means unique, as some overlap between the work of all security agencies is inevitable.

Uniform and Insignia

The official uniform of the Geheime Feldpolizei was the field grey of the Army administrative officials (Heeresbeamten) with the following distinctions:

Collar patches: dark green, bearing normal *Litzen*, with *Graublau* (grey-blue) arm of service piping (also used by Army Justice officials) on three edges (not forward edge). *Shoulder Straps*: standard Heeresbeamten straps, with *Graublau* piping and the monogram 'GFP' in stamped white metal letters. This monogram was also used on standard Army straps by auxiliaries on temporary attachment to the GFP. *Cuffband*: a black woven cuffband exists cm wide, bearing the legend '*Geheime Feldpolizei*' in woven aluminium thread Gothic script. Intended for wear on the lower left sleeve, it is uncertain if this piece of insignia ever saw general issue.

Warrant disc: a series of warrant discs was introduced for German Police personnel. Two such types, those for the KriPo (Criminal Police—*Staatliche Kriminal Polizei*) and GeStaPo (*Geheime Staats Polizei*—Secret State Police) are fairly well known to collectors. The GFP disc, however, is much rarer and of a different style. Round rather than oval, it carries on the face the Army rather than the State national emblem. The reverse carries the legend '*Oberkommando des Heeres*' in block Latin script around the upper edge and '*Geheime/Feldpolizei*' in two lines in the centre. Below this is the bearer's number. The disc is struck in silver-coloured metal.

Although little is recorded about the activities of the GFP, at least two of its personnel served with sufficient distinction to be awarded the German Cross in Silver (awarded for meritorious conduct rather than combat gallantry): Oberfeldpolizeidirektor Dr. Roman Loos, whose appointment was *Leitender Feldpol. Direktor*, *Oberbefehlshaber Südost*; and Heeresfeldpolizeimeister Karl Ziegler.

Other Army Police Services

Headquarter Guards

Personnel assigned to guard duties at headquarter buildings were issued with an identifying gorget from 1937 onwards. It was of identical construction to the Bahnhofswache gorget (described below), bearing the unit number in the centre; in this case, however, the scroll bore the legend '*Kommandantur*' in Gothic script.

These Headquarter Guards had considerable authority within their own areas. One friend of the author, a former SS-Unterscharführer in the 'Leibstandarte Adolf Hitler', recalled being arrested by a young *leutnant* of Kommandantura troops accompanied by a junior NCO. Having produced his papers on request he was told that they were not happy with them, and was escorted to the Berlin Kommandantura, where he was held in the cells for over 13 hours. Only by causing such a commotion as to become a real nuisance was he able to persuade his captors to contact the 'Leibstandarte's' Lichterfelde barracks, where the duty NCO was able to vouch for him and arrange his release, but without any apology for his unwarranted arrest. The arrest of a member of the Waffen-SS in the home town of

Feldgendarmerie tactical vehicle markings. The standard insignia used was a rectangular box mounted on two 'wheels' indicating the motorised nature of these troops. In the first type was a cross and letter 'O' above, for Ordnungstruppe. The more common type featured in the centre a stylised traffic wand. These insignia would be painted in black on light-coloured vehicles and in white on dark-painted vehicles, usually painted on the left wing. The Feldgendarmerie of the 'Hermann Göring' formations used a white disc bearing the letters 'Fg' in blue.

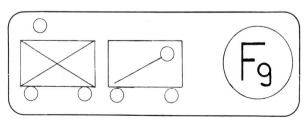

Hitler's élite 'Leibstandarte', and his rather cavalier treatment, shows that these Kommandantura guards were by no means shy of using their authority in any case where they felt justified in doing so.

Heeresstreifendienst

The Army Patrol Service was tasked with maintaining order and discipline in garrison areas (including occasional traffic control duties). No special insignia were introduced for these troops, but a duty lanyard was worn and special ID was carried. Patrols had authority over all Army personnel (including administrative officials) in their areas, with the exception of officers of general rank. Any offenders could be reported by the patrol to the military authority responsible for the soldier or, if this was too distant, the patrol could specify punishment and have it carried out by the nearest competent authority. Any soldier found without proper identification could be arrested by the patrol and escorted to his unit for punishment.

Soldiers in the area could be called upon to assist the Heeresstreifendienst in the execution of its duties and failure to assist was a punishable offence. Patrols were armed with machine-pistols and could use these to maintain good order and discipline if the situation was regarded as serious. Like all military policemen, the Heeresstreifendienst were expected to carry out their tasks with tact but firmness, and show a good example to other troops. The Luftwaffe and Kriegsmarine also had street patrols, but all were combined in 1941 to become the Wehrmachtstreifendienst, and formalised training was established in 1943.

Bahnhofswache

The Bahnhofswache were soldiers responsible for policing large rail centres. Among their duties were the checking of travel papers and identity documents, directing military personnel, and generally assisting in the security and smooth flow of traffic. Bahnhofswache were also used to screen train passengers, hunting for deserters or soldiers absent without leave.

Gorget of Zugwachabteilung 502. This basic style is very similar to that of the Feldgendarmerie. All of the insignia are attached to the backplate by flat prongs. (F. J. Stephens)

As a badge of office, Bahnhofswache troops wore a light metal gorget similar to that worn by the Feldgendarmerie, being a half-moon shaped sheet of stamped metal with a rolled edge. In the centre was a Roman numeral indicating the *Wehrkries* or Military District number above an Arabic numeral indicating the unit number. Both these numerals, in luminous finish, were sited above a dark grey scroll bearing the luminous inscription '*Bahnhofswache*' in Gothic script. In each corner was a closed wing eagle, also in luminous finish. The gorget was suspended around the neck with a plain link chain identical to that used on the Feldgendarmerie gorget. The reverse was normally covered in a field grey cloth. As an alternative to the gorget an armband could be worn; it was in yellow cloth with the legend '*Bahnhofswache*' in black Latin script.

The gorget of the Royal Hungarian Gendarmerie. Obviously of German manufacture, it is stamped from aluminium and has its features rivetted rather than attached by prongs. It has no luminous finish. See Plate D3.

Zugwache

The Zugwache were Army troops assigned for duty to police military trains and rail centres through which large bodies of troops passed. Their duties included the maintenance of order and discipline, escorting trains used by High Command Staff, and guarding trains passing through enemy territory. As the war progressed and partisan activity and sabotage increased, the Zugwache troops became essential to safe troop movements.

As a badge of office, the Zugwache troops wore a duty gorget, similar to that of the Bahnhofswache. In the centre was the monogram 'WB' ('Wach Bataillon') over an Arabic numeral denoting the unit number. The scroll bore the legend '*Zugwache*' in Gothic script. A variation of this gorget exists having only a number and no monogram in the centre, and the legend '*Zugwachabteilung*' on the scroll. As with the Bahnhofswache, an armband could be worn in lieu of the gorget.

* * *

Hungarian Gendarmerie

These troops were not, of course, German personnel, but are mentioned here because they fought alongside their German allies on the Eastern Front and wore a German-made gorget similar to that of the Feldgendarmerie.

The Hungarian Gendarmerie was originally formed in 1881, and during the Second World War fought with the Royal Hungarian Army, wearing standard army uniform with a distinctive large blue-green feather on the cap, and a duty gorget. The Gendarmerie carried out security and anti-partisan duties, gaining a fearsome reputation. By late 1944 the Royal Hungarian Gendarmerie fielded five full divisions in the defence of Budapest.

The Hungarian Gendarmerie gorget was of identical shape to that of the Feldgendarmerie but was struck in aluminium. In place of the 'corner' buttons were two small rivets to each side. In the centre was the Royal Hungarian coat of arms over a scroll with the legend '*Tábori Biztonsag*' (Field Security) or '*Csendör*' (Gendarme). On the reverse was an issue number. The gorget was suspended around the neck by a plain link chain identical to that of the Feldgendarmerie.

Waffen-SS Feldgendarmerie

The Feldgendarmerie of the Waffen-SS was a much smaller organisation than its Army counterpart, but fulfilled identical functions. Like the Army Military Policeman, the Waffen-SS Feldgendarme was more than likely a former civil policeman or an experienced combat NCO with around four years' service.

Each field division of the Waffen-SS had its Feldgendarmerie unit. For example the 'Leibstandarte Adolf Hitler' received its Feldgendarmerie-trupp in 1940 when it was expanded to Brigade status. The Feldgendarmerietrupp consisted of one officer, four NCOs and 36 men. Vehicle status was one Volkswagen 'Kubelwagen' jeep and 11 motorcycle combinations. When the 'Leibstandarte' was expanded to divisional strength in 1942 its Feldgendarmerie unit was enlarged to a *Kompanie*; this consisted of three platoons (*Zuge*) each of approximately the same strength as the previous Feldgendarmerietrupp.

Photographic records of Waffen-SS Feldgendarmerie are relatively rare. It is probable that they were used primarily to maintain order and discipline within their own unit lines, and their areas of responsibility were thus more restricted than those .of the Army Feldgendarmerie. One Waffen-SS veteran, SS-Unterscharführer Erwin Bartmann of the 'Leibstandarte', recalled that despite serving with the 'LAH' throughout the whole war, he never came across a single Waffen-SS Feldgendarme, only those from the Army. As the Feldgendarmerie were divisional troops, it is quite possible that a combat NCO in an infantry section might never meet up with such personnel, but would encounter their Army counterparts on many occasions.

Uniforms and Insignia

Until the introduction of a special SS pattern cuffband in 1942, SS-Feldgendarmen wore the standard woven pattern Army cuffband previously described. The SS pattern band was woven in black rayon with a woven metallic silver thread edging. The legend '*SS-Feldgendarmerie*' was woven into the band in grey artificial silk Latin script. This was not a so-called 'Bevo' cuffband, but similar to an RZM issue type with woven script. The SS pattern cuffband was withdrawn in 1944.

From 1942 until 1944 the SS pattern sleeve eagle was to have been replaced with the type used by the Army. This rarely seems to have been adhered to, however, as most photographic material shows the SS sleeve eagle to have been worn throughout the

SS-Feldgendarmerie on the Eastern Front. These men are from 3.SS-Panzer-Grenadier-Division 'Totenkopf'. The Stabsscharführer holding the field telephone handset wears the duty gorget and Army-pattern 'Feldgendarmerie' cuffband. (Munin Verlag)

Above: A Stabsscharführer of 'Totenkopf' Division SS-Feldgendarmerie interrogates a suspect with his platoon commander, an SS-Untersturmführer, watching the proceedings. The NCO wears the Schirmmutze without chinstrap, the officer apparently the 'old style officer's field cap'. (Munin Verlag)

Below: An SS-Unterscharführer and SS-Rottenführer of 'Totenkopf' Division Feldgendarmerie check a motorcyclist's papers. Note the whistle lanyard on the Unterscharführer's tunic pocket. Both wear the duty gorget. The motorcycle sidecar bears the emblem of the division. (Munin Verlag)

The SS-Pattern Feldgendarmerie cuffband, of the standard RZM type pattern but with machine-woven lettering rather than embroidered. Use of this cuffband seems to have been limited as most photographs show the Army pattern being worn. (B. L. Davis)

war. On the shoulder straps and as piping on headgear, the SS-Feldgendarme wore the same orange-red Waffenfarbe as his Army counterpart.

From October 1944 onwards, former members of the *Ordnungspolizei* serving with the Waffen-SS (and many of these would be in the SS-Feldgendarmerie) could wear as a special distinction a small diamond-shaped patch on the lower left sleeve depicting the Polizei-style eagle and swastika in silver grey thread.

The Waffen-SS had no Geheime Feldpolizei units, though these would hardly have been necessary to the SS, which encompassed such organisations as the Sicherheitsdienst and Gestapo under its control.

Although the Feldgendarmerie of the Waffen-SS was a rather small organisation, the Waffen-SS did boast two actual combat divisions of Police troops. Although the second division, formed late in the war, barely reached regimental strength, the first was a fully equipped combat division which fought

The final pattern 'Bevo' SS-Polizei-Division cuffband introduced in 1943, woven in black artificial silk with silver-grey edges and lettering. The 'chequerboard' effect on the reverse is typical of Bevo woven SS cuffbands.

throughout the whole war and included several highly decorated soldiers in its ranks. Although not Military Police in the Provost sense, these men were Police troops and did fight at the front as combat soldiers, and so were certainly Military Police in the strict sense of the term.

4.SS-Polizei-Panzer-Grenadier-Division

This division was raised in October 1939 from former Ordnungspolizei—civilian policemen and Allgemeine-SS reservists. Commanded initially by Generalleutnant Karl Pfeffer-Wildenbruch, the Division was still working up when Poland was invaded, but it did see some occupation duties in Poland before the opening of the Western campaign. After the fall of France it remained in the West until the attack on the Soviet Union in 1941. The division was allocated to *Armee Gruppe Nord* and took part in the advance on Leningrad. Rather poorly trained and equipped, its performance was uneven. It was involved in heavy combat around Wolchow and Lake Ladoga, where it acquitted itself well but suffered heavy losses.

From spring until summer 1943, the division was used for anti-partisan duties in the protectorate of Bohemia-Moravia (Czechoslovakia) and in Jugo-slavia, where it took part in the ferocious struggle against Tito's partisan forces, little quarter being given on either side. In March 1944 the division

moved into Greece, where once again it was used for security duties; divisional personnel committed atrocities in the Larissa area. Late 1944 found the Polizei Division in Hungary taking part in the defensive battles against the Red Army, before being transferred once again to the northern sector of the front. After suffering heavy losses in the fighting around Danzig the division was pulled back for the defence of Berlin, where it was finally destroyed. Its final commander was the Arnhem veteran SS-Standartenführer Walter Harzer. Among the most highly decorated members of the division were the following:

SS-Hauptsturmführer Heinz Jürgens

Heinz Jürgens was born in Miltzow, Pomerania on 21 March 1917, and commenced his military career with 1/SS-Regiment 'Germania' in Hamburg in 1937. After attending the SS-Junkerschule at Bad Tölz he was promoted to SS-Untersturmführer and posted to the Berlin police. On the outbreak of war he joined the SS-Polizei Division and served in its recce squadron during the campaign in the West, being seriously wounded in France. In June 1940 he

Men of the SS Polizei Division watch with satisfaction the raising of the German flag over an occupied Soviet town, 1941. Note the Polizei-pattern collar patches being worn in conjunction with the SS sleeve eagle. Polizei-type field caps are being worn, together with SS issue camouflage clothing.

was promoted to Oberleutnant der Schutzpolizei. With the recce squadron he took part in the attack on Russia, and saw action at Wolchow and Leningrad. In January 1942 he was awarded the Iron Cross 1st Class and promoted to SS-Hauptsturmführer and Hauptmann der Schutzpolizei. During August 1944 he took command of 4 Polizei Panzer Aufklärungs Abteilung and served in this capacity during the division's actions in Hungary and Czechoslovakia from September 1944 to January 1945. On 6 January 1945 he was awarded the German Cross in Gold.

When involved in the defence of Danzig a Soviet breakthrough fragmented the division and some units found themselves being used as a 'fire brigade' under Von Manteuffel's 5 Panzerarmee. Jürgens, with his recce battalion and various attached elements, totalling around 2,000 men, was in defence of the bridgehead at Langenberg. For four weeks he and his men held out against overwhelm-

SS-Hauptsturmführer Heinz Jürgens, commander of SS-Polizei-Panzer-Aufklärungsabteilung 4, was decorated with the Knight's Cross on 8 May 1945. By this stage SS-Polizei-Division personnel were wearing full Waffen-SS uniforms and insignia. (Heinz Jürgens)

ing odds. Strong Soviet forces with heavy artillery and armoured support threw themselves at the German positions, Jürgens' reece unit taking the brunt of the attack; despite everything the Soviets could throw at them the German positions held. Jürgens was highly commended for his actions, and the Commander-in-Chief of XXXII Armee Korps praised the bravery and leadership shown during these ferocious battles in an Army Order of the Day. On 8 May 1945 Heinz Jürgens was decorated with the Knight's Cross of the Iron Cross. Jürgens' final rank was SS-Hauptsturmführer and Major der Schutzpolizei. He was still alive at the time of writing.

SS-Hauptsturmführer Hans Traupe

Hans Traupe was born on 4 May 1913 in Kunern, the son of an agricultural official. His career began in 1934 when he joined the Army's Infanterie Regiment 71. His military service completed in

1936, he volunteered for the SS-Verfügungstruppe After attending the SS-Junkerschule at Bad Tölz he was commissioned as a Leutnant der Schutz-polizei and posted to the Berlin police. Joining the SS-Polizei Division on the outbreak of war, Traupe served with the division throughout the opening stages of Operation 'Barbarossa', winning the German Cross in Gold in September 1942.

In January 1944 the Soviet counter-attacks on the Leningrad front broke through the German lines and several elements of 18.Armee were in danger of being encircled. Traupe and his battalion held the retreat route open for several days of intense combat against overwhelming odds, thus allowing many German units to avoid encircle-ment. Traupe was awarded the Knight's Cross of

SS-Obersturmbannführer Hans Traupe, another of the Polizei-Division's Knight's Cross winners. Also a Close Combat Clasp winner, Traupe won the Knight's Cross in February 1944; he ended the war with the 10. SS-Panzer Division 'Frundsberg'. (Hans Traupe)

he Iron Cross on 23 October 1944. Sent to the Panzertruppenschule of the Army in Fallingbostel for training as a regimental commander, Traupe was subsequently posted to 10.SS Panzer Division 'Frundsberg' as commander of Panzer Grenadier Regiment 20.

SS-Hauptsturmführer Johannes Scherg

Johannes Scherg was born on 16 May 1918 in Würzburg. On completing his obligatory service with the Reichsarbeitsdienst in 1938 he joined the SS-Verfügungstruppe in Munich, and was accepted in the SS-Regiment 'Deutschland'. At the outbreak of war Scherg was a signaller in the armoured recce troop of the regiment, and served in the Polish and Western campaigns.

In May 1941 Scherg began an officer training

SS-Hauptsturmführer Johannes Scherg, who was decorated with the Knight's Cross when commanding 1 Kompanie of Polizei-Panzer-Aufklärungsabteilung 4 in October 1944. Note that he wears the Close Combat Clasp and the Panzer Assault Badge as well as the cloth embroidered version of the German Cross in gold (Johannes Scherg)

course at Bad Tölz; and in October of that year was commissioned as an SS-Untersturmführer. Posted as a platoon commander to the recce platoon of 1. Kompanie, SS-Aufklärungs Abteilung 2 'Das Reich', Scherg went into action on the central sector of the Eastern Front during Operation 'Barbarossa'. After gaining valuable combat experience Scherg eventually took command of 2.Kompanie of the Abteilung; in November 1943 he was decorated with the German Cross in Gold and promoted to Obersturmführer. In July 1944 Scherg was posted to command 1.Kompanie, Panzer Aufklärungs Abteilung 4 in the SS-Polizei Division.

During the division's participation in the defensive actions against the Soviets in late 1944, contact with Scherg and his company was lost. Despite orders to retreat in the face of heavy Soviet armoured forces, Scherg waited, holding back the Soviets and giving the units on his flanks time to withdraw to safety. Scherg then made his own breakout and reached safety with all his men, including the wounded. On 23 October 1944 Scherg was decorated with the Knight's Cross of the Iron Cross for his achievements. On 30 January 1945 he was promoted to Hauptsturmführer. At the conclusion of the war Scherg was captured by British troops at Lauenberg on the Elbe on 14 May 1945. He was eventually taken into French captivity, where he remained until 1951.

35.SS-Polizei-Grenadier-Division

One of a number of Waffen-SS 'divisions' formed in the closing stages of the war, many of which never reached more than regimental strength, this unit was raised in February 1945 from the staff of the Dresden Polizeischule and some personnel from the SS-Junkerschule (Officer Training Academy) Braunschweig. It served on the Niesse front in regimental strength in the closing stages of the war, and surrendered to the Soviets at Halbe, east of Prague in May 1945.

Many adverse comments have been made about the quality of the SS Police troops. Whilst it is true they never reached the level of the élite SS Divisions such as the 'Leibstandarte' or 'Das Reich', and that they were often equipped to a poor standard, the 4.SS-Polizei-Division, at least, acquitted itself on occasion with some merit, and numbered at least 15 Knight's Cross winners among its personnel.

Uniforms and Insignia

Members of the SS-Polizei-Division initially wore a combination of SS and Police uniforms and insignia. Standard Army or Waffen-SS field dress was worn with the standard SS sleeve eagle on the left sleeve. Shoulder straps were piped in 'Police green' Waffenfarbe; and Army or Police style collar patches were worn, also with Police green Waffenfarbe. In February 1942 the formation was fully absorbed into the Waffen-SS, and thereafter full SS insignia and rank badges were worn. Headgear, initially of Polizei pattern, was also changed for normal SS issue.

Members of the SS Police Division wore a divisional cuffband. Initially this comprised a black rayon band with silver wire weave edges and a woven representation of the Police pattern wreathed eagle and swastika. In December 1942 a new pattern was introduced in the same style of manufacture bearing the legend '*SS-Polizei Division*' in silver wire weave or hand embroidery for officers, and silver-grey machine-embroidered thread for other ranks. In 1943 an all-machine-woven pattern was introduced for all ranks with the legend in silver grey weave. Many photographs from various stages of the division's development show troops wearing no cuffband, however.

Pre-enlistment members of the SS serving in the Police wore silver-embroidered SS runes on a field grey backing on the left breast pocket of the tunic. During the early stages of the division's history, when the Police-style insignia were being worn, this runic insignia was commonly seen.

* * *

Italian SS-Feldgendarmerie

There is little reliable information available on the uniforms and insignia of the Italian SS units, and even less on their Feldgendarmerie. Photographs of personnel from 29.Waffen-Grenadier-Division der SS show a mixture of Italian uniforms and Italian and SS insignia being worn. Initially the Italian SS insignia was embroidered on a red backing, but in June 1944 the backing was changed to black. At least one example of a special pattern of gorget for the Italian SS-Feldgendarmerie exists. The central motif in this case is the SS-style eagle bearing fasces in its talons in place of the swastika; the scroll bears the legend '*Gendarmeria*'.

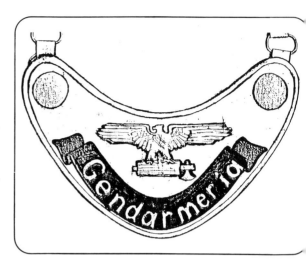

Line drawing based on an original example of the special gorget pattern for Feldgendarmerie of the Italian Waffen-SS troops. Although it closely resembles the German gorget this pattern features the SS-style eagle bearing the fasces in its talons, and the legend 'Gendarmeria' rather than Feldgendarmerie.

Luftwaffe Police

Luftwaffe Feldgendarmerie

Of the three Feldgendarmerie organisations, that of the Luftwaffe was the smallest. Only the ground combat units of the Luftwaffe had Feldgendarmerie components. These included the Luftwaffen Feld Divisionen, Fallschirmjäger Divisionen, and the Fallschirmpanzerkorps 'Hermann Göring'. Each division would have an attached Feldgendarmerie trupp.

The largest of the Luftwaffe ground formations was the 'Hermann Göring' Division (later, Korps) and thus within this formation was to be found the Luftwaffe's largest Feldgendarmerie element. Within the 'Hermann Göring' Korps, there existed three Feldgendarmerie units: Feldgendarmerie trupp Fallschirmpanzerkorps 'Hermann Göring; Feldgendarmerietrupp Fallschirmpanzer Division 'Hermann Göring 1'; Feldgendarmerietrupp Fallschirmpanzer Division 'Hermann Göring 2'. Each Trupp would typically have had the following components:

HQ element: Unit commander (Leutnant or Hauptmann), deputy commander (Leutnant or Warrant Officer), three–five Unteroffiziere (interpreters), three–five men (drivers and orderlies)

1: NCO, Feldgendarmerie, 1939
2: Officer, Geheime Feldpolizei, 1939
3: SS-Oberscharführer, 4.SS-Polizei-Div., 1940

Umleitung

A

1: Hauptfeldwebel, Feldgendarmerie, 1940
2: SS-Unterscharführer, Feldgendarmerie, 1940-41
3: Oberwachtmeister, Polizei-Schutzen-Regt., 1941

B

1: Warrant officer, Marine Küstenpolizei, 1939
2: Feldpolizeiinspektor, Luftwaffe GFP, 1943
3: Warrant officer, Marine Küstenpolizei, 1943

C

1: Hauptmmann, Feldgendarmerie, 1941
2: Gefreiter, Signals, 1941
3: Sergeant, Royal Hungarian Gendarmerie, 1944

D

1: Leutnant, Feldgendarmerie; N. Africa, 1941
2: Oberfeldwebel, Feldgendarmerie; N. Africa, 1942
3: SS-Feldgendarme, 29.W-Gren.-Div. der SS, 1944

E

1: Hauptmann, Feldgendarmerie, 'Hermann Göring' Korps, 1944-45
2: NCO, Feldgendarmerie, Fallschirmtruppen; Normandy, 1944
3: Obergefreiter, Feldgendarmerie, 'Hermann Göring' Div., 1944

F

1: SS-Untersturmführer, Feldgemdarmerie, 2.SS-PzGren.-Div., 1943
2: Unterfeldwebel, Feldgendarmerie, 1944
3: Feldwebel, Feldgendarmerie, 1944-45

Bahnhof

G

1: SS-Scharführer, Feldgendarmerie, 1945
2: Hauptfeldwebel, Feldjäger, 1945
3: Feldwebel, Feldgendarmerie, summer 1945

H

× *Platoons*: Platoon commander (Warrant Officer), three Oberfeldwebel (patrol commanders), 12 Unteroffiziere five men (drivers and orderlies).

Support Group: one each Warrant Officer (Sergeant Major), Chief Clerk Oberfeldwebel, Armourer Oberfeldwebel, MT Oberfeldwebel, Supplies Oberfeldwebel, Quartermaster Oberfeldwebel (Clothing), three–five Unteroffizier (admin. and supply clerks), five–ten men as mechanics, drivers, medics and orderlies. Each Trupp would have a total strength of around 100 officers, NCOs and men.

Officers and warrant officers were mainly career soldiers who had come from the Prussian Landespolizei (via 'Landespolizeigruppe z.b.V. Wecke', and Regiment 'General Göring') and the Motorisierten Gendarmerie. NCOs and men were mostly career soldiers and conscripts. The Musikkorps 'Hermann Göring' was absorbed into the Feldgendarmerie in 1944.

The Feldgendarmerie of the Luftwaffe field units was under the direct control of the divisional command. The duties of the Luftwaffe Feldgendarmerie were similar to those of their Army and Waffen-SS counterparts. Particularly important was the securing and patrolling of the division's supply routes, prevention of sabotage and anti-partisan patrols. Feldgendarmerie were fully motorised but with only light unarmoured vehicles and light weapons (though Panzerfaust anti-tank projectiles were issued in the latter part of the war). Feldgendarmerie often found themselves in direct contact with enemy forces. Luftwaffe Feldgendarmerie were of course responsible for the maintenance of order and discipline within their divisions, and for the assistance of the military justice system. (For the latter, only those with former civil police experience were used.) The maintenance of order and security in rearward sections of the divisional

A rare shot of a Luftwaffe Field Court Martial in Sicily in 1943; the placard on the Opel Blitz truck reads 'Feldgericht der Luftwaffe'. Note that the vehicle is well camouflaged against enemy air attack. (Herbert Kail)

areas was carried out by the Feldgendarmerie platoons using traffic posts on all important road junctions, to regulate traffic flow and protect it from partisan attack. Permanent traffic and information posts were also located at divisional headquarters. Luftwaffe Feldgendarmerie also operated immediately behind the front line to collect stragglers and fragmented units and redirect them.

During the retreat through Poland in 1945 when units of the 'Hermann Göring' formations were encircled, the despatch riders of the 'Hermann Göring' Feldgendarmerie carried out many dangerous night missions through the Soviet lines to escort precious fuel supply vehicles to the beleagured 'Hermann Göring' troops.

Uniforms and Insignia

The Waffenfarbe of the Luftwaffe Feldgendarme was initially light-blue, this being the colour for Luftwaffe Verwaltungstruppe (Administrative

Troops) of which the Feldgendarmerie wa considered a part. In 1943, however, this wa changed to conform with the orange-red of the Army and Waffen-SS Feldgendarmerie. Thi Waffenfarbe was worn as piping or underlay or shoulder straps and as piping on NCOs' and men collar patches of the 'Hermann Göring' units up to April 1943. Strictly speaking, the Waffenfarbe wa the only identifying insignia of the Luftwaffe Feldgendarme if the duty gorget was not being worn. It has been confirmed, however, by veteran of the 'Hermann Göring' Division that forme civilian policemen serving in the division's Feldgen darmerietrupp wore the Army-pattern '*Feldgendar merie*' cuffband on the left sleeve. This is supported by photographic evidence reproduced here.

A special Luftwaffe version of the Feldgendar merie gorget has been known for some time from a few surviving original examples in private col lections. This differed from the standard Feldgen darmerie gorget in that it featured a Luftwaffe pattern 'flying' eagle. However, most surviving photographs of Luftwaffe Feldgendarmerie show

Unteroffizier Herbert Kail, a Luftwaffe Feldgendarme serving with the Court Martial branch, at his desk 'in the field'. (Herbert Kail)

'Hermann Göring' Division Feldgendarmen, Sicily, 1943. The 'Hermann Göring' cuffband can just be seen on the right sleeve of Unteroffizier Kail, left. Only the shoulder strap piping shows the branch of service on this particular form of dress. Of special interest are the so-called 'Hermann Meyer' tropical field caps being worn, and the tropical-style collar Tresse on Kail's tunic. (Herbert Kail)

hat the Army pattern gorget was almost always worn. Confirmation in both testimony and photographic evidence from the same veterans now shows that at least within the 'Hermann Göring' Korps, the special Luftwaffe version was certainly worn. The small number used, and the fact that the bulk of the 'Hermann Göring' units went into Soviet captivity, probably explains the rarity of these gorgets. It is probably true that at least some other Luftwaffe ground units used this gorget, however, as at least one example in a private collection was 'liberated' in France in 1944.

(It is also known that some Luftwaffe units wore field grey uniforms, as opposed to the normal field blue from late 1944 onwards.)

Unteroffizier Herbert Kail from Feldgendarmerietrupp Fallschirmpanzerkorps 'Hermann Göring' on horseback, East Prussia, 1944. The use of horses was because of the congested state of the roads, making the usual Kubelwagen transport rather difficult. Note that the Luftwaffe-pattern gorget is being worn. (Herbert Kail)

Luftwaffe Geheime Feldpolizei

The Luftwaffe formed its own Geheime Feldpolizei in 1943. Its tasks were identical to those of its Army counterparts, but of course were concerned with Luftwaffe matters. Luftwaffe Geheime Feldpolizei wore normal Luftwaffe service dress with the following special insignia.

Collar Patches: Standard Luftwaffe patches, in dark green cloth bearing the following designs. *Feldpolizeisekretär*—green/silver twist edging; three-point embroidered silver star over silver oakleaf cluster. *Feldpolizeiobersekretär*—green/silver twist edging; two three-point embroidered silver stars over silver oakleaf cluster. *Feldpolizei Inspektor*—silver twist edging; two three-point silver embroidered stars over silver oakleaf cluster. *Feldpolizei Kommisar*—silver twist edging. Three three-point silver embroidered stars over silver oakleaf cluster. *Feldpolizei Direktor*—gilt twist edging; one three-point star within oakleaf wreath. *Oberfeldpolizei Direktor*—gilt twist edging; two three-point stars within oakleaf wreath.

Shoulder straps: Standard Luftwaffe *Beamten* shoulder straps with the following distinctions. *Feldpolizeisekretär*—dark green base, wine red Waffenfarbe, flat silver braid with gilt letters 'GFP'. *Feldpolizeiobersekretär*—as above but with one gilt rank pip. *Feldpolizei Inspektor*—as above. *Feldpolizei Kommisar*—as above but with two gilt rank pips. *Feldpolizei Direktor*—dark green base, wine red Waffenfarbe, twisted silver braid with gilt letters 'GFP'. *Oberfeldpolizei Direktor*—as above plus one gilt rank pip.

No special cuffband was introduced for the Luftwaffe Geheime Feldpolizei.

Marine Kustenpolizei

The Kriegsmarine possessed no Feldgendarmerie of its own as such, but in common with most other navies it did have a Provost organisation similar to the shore patrols of the British and US Navies. This was the Marine Küstenpolizei, whose duties included guarding coastal defences and maintaining order and discipline in coastal towns where naval personnel were located. As with the Police formations of the Luftwaffe, Army and Waffen-SS,

Despatch rider Wolfgang Dinger from Feldgendarmerietrupp Fallschirmpanzerdivision 1 'Hermann Göring'. The special Luftwaffe-pattern gorget is being worn. Also of interest is that the uniform is in Army Feldgrau and not the Feldblau of the Luftwaffe. (Wolfgang Dinger)

The Marine Küstenpolizei gorget, unusual in that it does not feature the eagle and swastika emblem; the lettering and buttons are in luminous finish while the plate itself is silver-grey.

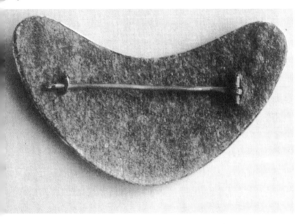

The reverse of the Marine Küstenpolizei gorget, unique among the military gorgets in that it does not have a neck chain: the long hinged pin passed through thread loops on the jacket lapels.

members of the Marine Küstenpolizei were generally former members of the civil Police, and his is reflected in the fact that the first pattern Marine Küstenpolizei uniform was almost identical to that of the Wasserschutzpolizei.

First pattern Uniform

Peaked cap: A traditional naval style cap with wide floppy crown and featuring either a white or blue cover. The cap band was black, and the cap had a plain black leather chinstrap and plain black gloss peak. Insignia consisted of a Polizei style eagle and swastika in gilt metal with a national cockade above.

Tunic: A double-breasted dark blue naval style 'reefer jacket' with gilt buttons and gilt piping to the cuffs. Water Police pattern shoulder straps on a gold-yellow base were worn, as was a Police pattern arm eagle in yellow thread (gold wire for officers) on a blue base on the left sleeve. A narrow dark blue cuffband with yellow braid edges was worn on the lower left sleeve, bearing the legend '*Marine Küstenpolizei*' in yellow Gothic script letters.

Second Pattern Uniform (introduced in 1940)

Peaked cap: A standard issue Kriegsmarine peaked cap, with a national emblem of the eagle and swastika on the crown, and a national cockade within a wreath of oakleaves on the capband. These insignia were generally in yellow thread for NCOs and gilt wire for officers. Additionally, officers showed their rank grading by gilt wire embroidery on a cloth base to the peak edge, in the same style as regular naval officers.

Tunic: A standard naval issue double-breasted jacket. Rank was shown by shoulder straps for NCOs and shoulder straps or sleeve rings for officers. No sleeve eagle was worn, but the standard yellow thread or gold wire naval breast eagle was applied.

For some reason the Marine Küstenpolizei based in Norway continued to wear the early-pattern uniform throughout the war.

A unique pattern of gorget was produced for these Naval Police troops. In the typical half-moon shape of the Feldgendarmerie gorget, it was much smaller, and devoid of any national emblem. The buttons featured on this gorget were of the standard 'fouled anchor' naval type. In the centre was the legend *Marine-Küsten/Polizei* in two lines of Latin script stamped into the metal, and not a separately fixed feature as with most gorgets. Also unusual was the lack of a neck chain; this gorget was held in place by a large hinged pin on the reverse which passed through thread loops stitched to the lapels of the jacket.

The Marine Küstenpolizei was the smallest of all the Military Police organisations.

Police Combat Units

The subject of the German Police during the period of the Third Reich is complex in the extreme. An

A rather cold-looking Oberfeldwebel from the Spanish 'Blue Division' on the Eastern Front in 1942, identified by his duty gorget and traffic wand. Of additional interest is the shield bearing the Spanish colours on the right sleeve. He is armed with the Walther P38 pistol (J. Charita)

enormous range of Police organisations existed— Schutzpolizei, Gendarmerie, Kriminalpolizei, Wasserschutzpolizei, Verkehrspolizei, Hochgebirgs Gendarmerie, Feuerschutzpolizei and Bahnschutzpolizei to name but a few. In this book we will concern ourselves only with the Police units which took part in combat operations.

The German Police was divided into two principal branches: the Sicherheitspolizei or Security Police and the Ordnungspolizei or Order Police. Within the Order Police the principal organisation was the Schutzpolizei or Protection Police, one of the many sub-branches of which was the Kasernierte Polizei or Barrack Police. These were quasi-military formations based in the larger towns. Kasernierte Polizei units developed from the Polizei Hundertschaften (100-strong units) of pre-war days, and had soon developed into battalion-

strength units of around 500 men which were under the control of the staff of the local Hohere SS und Polizei Führung (Higher SS and Police Leadership).

Polizei units (of battalion and later regimenta strength) quickly followed Army combat units intc occupied territory. The Army could ill afford the manpower required to maintain order and prevent terrorism—especially during the invasion of the Soviet Union, where the initial welcome found by German Army units in many areas soon developec into hatred due to Hitler's idiotic racial policies, anc the general brutality visited upon the occupiec populations.

Due to the very fluid nature of the war on the Eastern Front, many Polizei units found themselve: in direct combat with Red Army units. The mos famous occasion was at Cholm, where large numbers of German troops, including Polizei, were encircled by Soviet forces. After the successful relie of the beleagured German troops a special award in the form of an arm shield was instituted tc commemorate the action. This shield was designec by Polizei Rottwachtmeister Schlimmer of the Reserve-Polizei-Bataillon Cholm.

By 1943 most of the Polizei-Bataillons had beer formed into regiments, of which approximately 4C saw action. As the Polizei was ultimately controllec by the SS, recruitment followed SS guidelines, anc many of those who joined the Polizei after 193! were fanatically loyal Nazis. The Polizei had its owr training schools, although use was also made of botl Army and Waffen-SS training establishments Polizei officers were trained at the SS Junkerschulen at Bad Tölz and Braunschweig being commissioned with dual Polizei and SS rank (i.e SS-Untersturmführer and Leutnant de Schutzpolizei.) It was possible for an officer's ris through the ranks to be at a different rate withir each organisation, so that an officer could becom e.g., SS-Hauptsturmführer (Captain) and Majo der Schutzpolizei.

In the sense that they were used principally fo

Many other organisations had their Police or Patrol securit services: the SA, NSDAP, SS etc all had their Streifendiens patrols. Shown here for the readers' interest is an excep tionally rare shot of a Flemish member of the Organisatio Todt Patrol Service. The gorget, of Army style, bears Political-pattern eagle, flanked by the letters 'O' and 'T' over scroll with the legend 'Streifendienst'. Note the SS runes wor on the tie, and the 'Flandern' arm shield. (J. Charita)

securing traffic routes, directing refugees, anti-partisan duties, etc, they shared a good deal of the work of the Feldgendarmerie. The Polizei combat units became notorious for the savagery with which they put down any partisan activities in their areas. Although officially part of the SS, these troops were not part of the Waffen-SS. These Polizei units were often greatly fragmented, with different battalions of the same regiment being found on different sectors of the front, or even on different fronts.

Uniforms and Insignia

Headgear: Several distinct patterns of headgear were worn by the Polizei combat units; the well-known Polizei shako was not one of them, however. The peaked cap or Schirmmütze worn by Schutzpolizei was of similar appearance to that of the Army, but with the capband in brown instead of dark green cloth. Piping was in 'Police green' Waffenfarbe. Insignia comprised a silver metal Polizei-pattern wreathed eagle and swastika on the band, with a national cockade above. An M43 Einheitsfeldmütze similar to the Army's was also worn, sometimes with green piping to the crown. The insignia on this cap was a one-piece machine-woven Polizei eagle and swastika in grey thread on field grey with a national cockade above. A Polizei-pattern sidecap was commonly used by Polizei combat troops. In field grey with green piping, this bore a machine-woven grey silk Polizei-pattern eagle and swastika on black backing. (Officers' caps were piped in silver and had the insignia machine woven in metallic thread.) The steel helmet worn by Polizei troops featured a black escutcheon bearing a silver-grey Polizei eagle and swastika on the right side just below the vent hole.
Tunics: The traditional tunic of the Schutzpolizei was in a field grey cloth of a distinctly greener shade than normal. The collar and cuffs were faced with brown cloth, and the cuffs each featured two silvered buttons. Both collar and cuffs were piped in 'Polizei green' Waffenfarbe. Standard Polizei-pattern shoulder straps and collar patches were used. The sleeve eagle on standard Schutzpolizei uniforms bore above its head the title of the town in which the unit was located; the field formations, however, wore the sleeve eagle without such a name. The eagle was in green machine-embroidered thread with the swastika in black

(machine-woven examples are known). Officers' examples were in hand-embroidered silver wire, but with the swastika still in black thread.

This standard pattern of tunic was certainly worn by field formations; but as the war progressed, much less elaborate versions were introduced, more in keeping with the style of tunic worn by Army and Waffen-SS troops. This type was in plain field grey cloth with no coloured facings. Lightweight greenish field grey denim tunics were also used during summer months or in hot weather. Camouflage clothing, when worn, was standard Waffen-SS issue.

Arms and equipment issued to these Polizei units were usually of obsolescent design, the newer equipment going to front line units of the Wehrmacht and Waffen-SS. (Even major units such as the SS-Polizei Divisions sometimes had to make do with obsolete or captured equipment.)

In the latter stages of the war, the Kasernierte Polizei even had its own tank troops. The Police Armoured units were equipped with old or captured equipment. The crews wore standard Army-pattern black Panzer uniforms, but with green piping to the tunic collar and Polizei rank insignia, sleeve eagle, etc.

The Plates

A1: NCO, Feldgendarmerie, 1939
This NCO from one of the first Feldgendarmerie units wears the uniform of the civil Gendarmerie but with Army badges of rank and breast eagle added. The field grey cloth used for Polizei uniforms had a distinctly greenish shade. The collar, cuffs and tunic front featured the orange piping of the Gendarmerie. As with the Schutzpolizei, Gendarmerie uniforms had brown facings to the collar and two-button cuffs. The forage cap, also piped in orange features an Army-pattern eagle and swastika. Grey-green long trousers are worn, with standard marching boots, and the NCO is armed with a PO8 pistol.

A2: Junior officer, Geheime Feldpolizei, 1939
As a member of the Heeresbeamten he wears the standard Army officer's field grey M36 *Feldbluse*

with dark green collar and officers'-pattern silver wire embroidered breast eagle. The shoulder straps are in matt grey braid on blue-grey underlay with a dark green base, and bear the gilt monogram 'GFP'. The officer-pattern collar *Litzen* in silver bullion are also on a dark green base and have grey-blue edge piping. The cuffband is speculative. Original examples survive but it is not known with any certainty whether these were actually issued. The field cap worn is the standard M38 pattern for officers, with silver braid piping. The chevron of *Waffenfarbe* over the cockade is the dark green of the Heeresbeamten.

A3: SS-Oberscharführer, 4.SS-Polizei-Division, 1940
The division saw its first important combat action during the invasion of France. This Oberscharführer wears the standard Army M36 *Feldbluse* for NCOs with silver braid *Tresse* to the collar edge. Army-type collar patches are used, with Police green *Waffenfarbe*. The shoulder straps are SS pattern in black cloth with silver braid NCO *Tresse*

Solemn-looking SS-Feldgendarmerie personnel from the 'Leibstandarte SS Adolf Hitler' interrogate captured Russian tank crewmen. The NCO wears the waterproof coat and has a signal torch attached by a small leather fob to the second button.

and Police green piping (though later, a whole range of *Waffenfarbe* colours was used). The single pip to the shoulder strap indicates his rank. A standard SS-pattern sleeve eagle is worn on the left upper arm. At this point in the division's history the cuffband was not in general use.

B1: Hauptfeldwebel, Feldgendarmerie, 1940
In 1940 the Army introduced its special Feldgendarmerie insignia. This Hauptfeldwebel in standard M36 combat dress has orange *Waffenfarbe* to his collar patches and shoulder straps. A Gendarmerie-type eagle is worn on the left sleeve, machine-embroidered in orange thread, while on the left cuff is worn the '*Feldgendarmerie*' cuffband in machine-woven artificial silk. From the neck is worn the Feldgendarmerie gorget or *Ringkragen*, soon to become the 'trademark' of the Feldgen-

41

darme. Above the cockade on the NCO's M38 cap is a Waffenfarbe chevron in orange. The Hauptfeld-webel wears the standard Army black leather belt carrying magazine pouches for his MP38 machine-pistol.

B2: SS-Unterscharführer, SS-Feldgendarmerie, 1940–41
Like most of the rest of the Waffen-SS the SS-Feldgendarmerie received Army issue clothing and, initially, partial Army insignia. This junior NCO wears the M36 *Feldbluse*; its dark green collar bears black patches with, on the right, the SS runes, and on the left the single silver pip of this rank. Black shoulder straps bear orange Waffenfarbe piping outside silver NCO *Tresse*. The SS sleeve eagle is worn, with an Army-pattern 'Feldgendarmerie' cuffband; the gorget is also of Army pattern. The

An SS-Feldgendarmerie Unterscharführer with feathered friend, Eastern Front. The Army-pattern Feldgendarmerie cuffband can be seen on the lower left sleeve. Note also the early-type Feldmütze with Totenkopf button. (Munin Verlag)

Army-pattern *Feldmütze* retains the Army form of national emblem, but the cockade has been covered by a metal SS *Totenkopf* insignia. The black leather belt supporting his holstered P38 has an SS buckle plate.

B3: Oberwachtmeister, Polizei-Schutzen-Regiment, 1941
Although Police Rifle Regiments eventually used uniforms more closely resembling those of the Army, early uniforms retained the brown Police collar and cuff facings. The green piping of the Schutzpolizei appears on the cuffs, collar, and tunic front, and there is a green underlay to the brown/silver braid Police shoulder straps. The Schutzpolizei arm eagle is embroidered in green and the *Litzen* on the collar patches are worked on a green base. Green piping also appears—in the unique Police arrangement, along the crown and down the front—on the Polizei-pattern *Feldmütze* which is of the '*Schiffchen*' shape also used by the Luftwaffe, Navy and Waffen-SS. A Polizei eagle

insignia, machine-woven in silver-grey thread on black, is sewn to the front of the flap. Army-type trousers and marching boots are worn. As 'second line' troops Polizei soldiers were often issued obsolete equipment, as with this NCO's MP28 Bergmann machine-pistol.

C1: Warrant Officer, Marine Küstenpolizei, 1939
The first pattern uniform was based upon that of the Wasserschutzpolizei. The double-breasted naval-style 'reefer' jacket has gilt buttons and also gold cuff-piping. A gilt wire embroidered Polizei-pattern sleeve eagle is worn on the left arm, and on the forearm the 'Marine Küstenpolizei' cuffband. The shoulder straps are of Wasserschutzpolizei pattern, as is the belt. Straight slacks are worn with black laced shoes. The naval-style peaked cap has a white summer crown cover, to which is fixed the national cockade, above a gilt Polizei eagle on the band.

C2: Feldpolizeiinspektor, Luftwaffe Geheime Feldpolizei, 1943
Personnel of this service were, like their Army counterparts, of 'Beamten' status. This officer, of a rank equivalent to captain, wears standard Luftwaffe officer's service dress differenced only by the green Beamten collar patches with their three-point stars instead of stylised wings; and the GFP shoulder straps, in bright silver braid on the characteristic double underlay of armed services officials, here wine red over dark green, with gilt (for officers) 'GFP' cyphers.

C3: Warrant officer, Marine Küstenpolizei, 1943
By the latter part of the war this service had adopted standard Kriegsmarine uniform in all respects. The small Marine Küstenpolizei gorget is attached by a pin through thread loops sewn to the jacket lapels.

D1: Hauptmann, Feldgendarmerie, 1941
This captain commanding a Feldgendarmerie-trupp on the Eastern Front wears the M36 officer's pattern Feldbluse. The orange-red branch-of-service colour features as 'lights' on the Litzen of his collar patches; as underlay to the oxidised-silver braid shoulder straps with their two gilt rank pips; and as piping on the crown and band of the Schirmmütze. The left sleeve eagle is in fine silver wire embroidery, as is the lettering on his privately purchased cuffband.

D2: Gefreiter, Signals Troops attached Feldgendarmerie, 1941
Soldiers from other branches of service could also be used as temporary Feldgendarmen. This soldier pressed into service on traffic duty wears standard uniform and equipment, with the lemon-yellow Waffenfarbe of Signals. His temporary authority is marked by the duty gorget, and by the special armband bearing 'Feldgendarmerie' in orange-yellow on a green background.

D3: Sergeant, Royal Hungarian Gendarmerie, 1944
The rather elaborate uniform of the Royal Hungarian Army bears rank insignia on the collar—a single star and strip of braid—and on the sleeve a single band of silver braid. This sergeant, in a service which earned itself a fearsome reputation in its areas of responsibility, wears a German M43 helmet, and a German-made gorget bearing the legend 'Csendör'.

E1: Leutnant, Feldgendarmerie; North Africa, 1941
This second lieutenant, newly arrived in Libya, wears the standard tropical Feldbluse, breeches, and Feldmütze in olive green cotton. The grey-blue and brown collar patches and blue on brown breast eagle were common to all ranks. Distinguishing insignia are the shoulder straps of rank on orange-red underlay, and the cuffband; the sleeve eagle and gorget are missing (the latter rarely worn by officers in any theatre of operations). Basic all-ranks cap insignia woven in silk are accompanied by a chevron of Waffenfarbe, and the silver piping showing officer's rank. The officer's pattern circular buckle is worn on the webbing belt. The lace-up leather and canvas boots were normal wear with the tropical breeches.

E2: Oberfeldwebel, Feldgendarmerie; North Africa, 1942
In sharp contrast, this seasoned desert veteran wears shirtsleeve order, shorts and ankle boots, with a Feldmütze bleached almost white by the sun and laundering. The shoulder straps of rank worn by non-commissioned ranks were of tropical pattern: of olive cotton, with rust-brown silk Tresse where appropriate, and the normal dull silver pips and Waffenfarbe piping. In this dress order the sleeve eagle and cuffband are obviously omitted. The web belt has the olive-painted enlisted ranks' buckle, and supports web magazine pouches for the MP38.

E3: SS-Feldgendarme, 29.Waffen-Grenadier-Division der SS, 1944

The Italian formation and units of the Waffen-SS wore a confusing variety of German and Italian uniforms and insignia. This MP wears the Italian steel helmet with SS rune decal insignia. His Italian Army tunic bears the Italian SS sleeve eagle, with the fasces replacing the swastika; and a standard SS rune collar patch—though a pattern bearing the fasces was also produced. The gorget is similar to the German model but bears the Italian SS eagle over the legend '*Gendarmeria*'. He is armed with a Beretta sub-machine gun.

F1: Hauptmann, Feldgendarmerie, Luftwaffe Fallschirm-panzerkorps 'Hermann Göring', 1944–45

Photographs of the Luftwaffe Feldgendarmerie are rare, but do indicate that dress generally followed that of the Luftwaffe field units. This captain of MPs

Eastern Front, 1944: Hauptman Barz and men of the Feldgendarmerietrupp Fallschirmpanzerkorps 'Hermann Göring'. Of particular interest in this photo is the use of the Army Feldgendarmerie cuffband by the driver of the Kubelwagen and by the Oberfeldwebel at extreme right. (Herbert Kail)

in the 'Hermann Göring' corps wears standard Luftwaffe officer's Schirmmütze and four-pocke tunic, with field-blue other ranks' trousers and ankle boots. Collar patches of rank have the white background of the 'Hermann Göring' units Waffenfarbe appearing only in the underlay to the shoulder straps. An experienced front line officer, he wears the Luftwaffe Ground Combat Badge and the Wound Badge in silver.

F2: Non-commissioned officer, Feldgendarmerie, Luft-waffe Fallschirmtruppen; Normandy, 1944

This battle-hardened military police NCO from a Luftwaffe parachute unit on the Normandy invasion front does not display any visible rank o branch insignia. His paratroop combat kit include: the special rimless helmet, its cover—and the jump smock—in 'splinter' camouflage material. The Army Feldgendarmerie gorget is the only visible indication of his MP status.

F3: Obergefreiter, Feldgendarmerie, Luftwaffe Fallschirm-panzerdivision 'Hermann Göring', 1944

By late 1944, when this largest Luftwaffe field

ormation was in the process of doubling (nominally) from divisional to corps strength, many of its personnel were wearing Army field-grey uniform due to shortages of field-blue issue. This junior NCO wears a field-grey M43 *Einheitsfeldmütze* with Luftwaffe insignia; the open-necked *Feldblüse* has four pleatless patch pockets, and bears the Luftwaffe breast eagle. On the right cuff is the 'Hermann Göring' cuffband, on the left the Army-pattern 'Feldgendarmerie' cuffband worn by former career policemen in the division's MP troop. His gorget is of the special Luftwaffe pattern with the 'flying eagle' national emblem.

G1: SS-Untersturmführer, SS-Feldgendarmerie, 2.SS-Panzer-Grenadier-Division 'Das Reich', 1943

The first of the wartime economy uniform patterns appeared in 1943; this second lieutenant wears the M43 tunic, with plain collar and unpleated pockets with straight flaps. The Waffen-SS officer's shoulder straps have the characteristic double underlay of Waffenfarbe (here, orange-red) on a black base. A hand-embroidered silver wire SS eagle is worn on the left sleeve; on the forearm, his divisional cuffband and the special 'SS-Feldgendarmerie' cuffband. Long field trousers, ankle boots, and a well-crushed Schirmmütze with orange-red piping complete the uniform. Note officers' pattern circular belt buckle.

G2: Unterfeldwebel, Feldgendarmerie, 1944

This veteran NCO shows the deterioration in the appearance of German uniform by 1944. His M43 tunic, with plain collar and pleatless pockets, is cut from much coarser cloth than formerly, with a smaller wool content. Collar patches are the same as those worn on the M36 tunic, but the shoulder straps are faced in field-grey rather than dark green cloth. Both the sleeve eagle and the cuffband have now been discarded. Marching boots have been replaced by ankle boots and canvas webbing anklets. The M43 'raw edge' helmet is covered here in Army splinter-pattern camouflage cloth.

G3: Feldwebel, Feldgendarmerie, 1944–45

The introduction of the M44 field uniform saw the final stage in the simplification and lowering of quality of German Army dress. As with the MPs of all nations, however, this NCO has made the effort

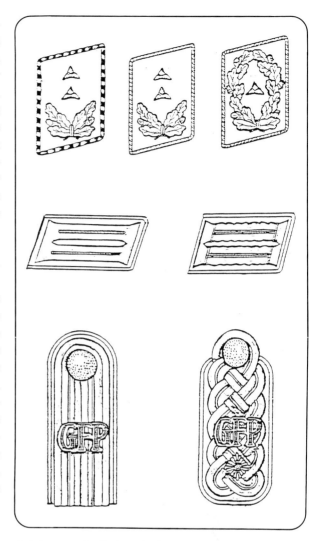

Geheime Feldpolizei insignia. The top row shows the Luftwaffe-style collar patches for the ranks of Feldpolizeiobersekretär, Feldpolizeiinspektor, and Feldpolizeidirektor. The central row shows the Army-style collar patches for rank gradings of Feldpolizeiassistent and Feldpolizeisekretär to Feldpolizeichef. Shoulder straps below are similar for both Luftwaffe and Army ranks of Feldpolizeisekretar and Oberfeldpolizeidirektor. Only colours used as described in the text differ.

to ensure as smart an appearance as possible. Sleeve eagle and cuffband are now absent; the collar patches, of 'field quality', are devoid of Waffenfarbe; only the shoulder strap piping and gorget still indicate branch of service. The headgear is the ubiquitous M43 *Einheitsfeldmütze*; he wears M44 trousers, and ankle boots with canvas anklets.

H1: SS-Scharführer, SS-Feldgendarmerie, 1945

This tough NCO, thrown into the front line with a small ad hoc *Kampfgruppe*, carries the Panzerfaust anti-tank projectile; previous success with this weapon is indicated by Tank Destruction Badges on his upper sleeve. As with G3, only the Waffenfarbe piping on his shoulder straps and the gorget now denote his MP status. His helmet cover is in Waffen-SS camouflage cloth; he is armed with a slung MP40 and stick grenades.

H2: Hauptfeldwebel, Feldjäger, 1945

This warrant officer of the dreaded Feldjäger shows a mixture of uniform items common at the end of the war. He wears the M43 helmet and tunic, but has been fortunate enough to retain good-quality marching boots. His Waffenfarbe is infantry white, and his long combat experience is indicated by the Infantry Assault Badge and Iron Cross 1st Class on his left pocket, and the Close Combat Clasp above. His gorget is of standard pattern except for the legend '*Feldjägerkorps*', and on his left forearm he wears the red brassard bearing the words '*Oberkommando der Wehrmacht/Feldjäger*'. His weapon is the latest SG44 assault rifle.

H3: Feldwebel, Feldgendarmerie, summer 1945

Germany's defeat left the Feldgendarmerie and Feldjäger formations among the last to lay down their arms. This NCO on traffic control duty well after VE-Day has been permitted to retain his pistol; but has removed the offending swastika from the breast eagle on his tunic, and the insignia from his M43 cap. He wears trousers made from Italian camouflage material, much in evidence as captured stocks were put to use following the Italian surrender.

Three Feldgendarmen from a Fallschirmjägerregiment in Normandy 1944. Although no longer employed as parachute-dropped infantry, such units still used the special Fallschirmjäger helmet. Note that the Army rather than the Luftwaffe-pattern gorget is worn here. (J. Charita)

Notes sur les planches en couleur

A1 Ce sous-officier porte l'uniforme de la Gendarmerie civile avec insignes de grade militaire et aigle sur la poitrine. Notez la couleur verte de l'uniforme de la Polizei et les parements bruns. **A2** Uniforme de base d'officier de l'armée, avec insignes dans le style des officiers des Heeresbeamten. Le ruban sur la manche existait, mais sa distribution et son port restent matière à spéculation. **A3** Notez le mélange d'insignes de col de type militaire, le Waffenfarbe en vert Polizei et l'aigle et les pattes d'épaule SS.

B1 Insignes de Feldgendarmerie—Waffenfarbe orange, aigle sur la manche du type de la Polizei, ruban sur le bras et plaque de col—furent introduits à partir de 1940. **B2** Col SS, patte d'épaule et insigne sur la manche de l'uniforme militaire, avec même liseré orange, ruban sur la manche et plaque de col que la Feld-Gendarmerie militaire; le Feldmütze de l'armée a simplement sa cocarde couverte par un écusson Totenkopf SS. **B3** Les premiers uniformes conservèrent la couleur et la coupe des uniformes de la police, ici avec le liseré vert de la Schutzpolizei, qui apparaît sur les manches et le devant de la vareuse de même que sur le col et les pattes d'épaule, ces dernières étant brunes et argent pour la police. Notez le liseré unique sur le calot de style police. Un équipement militaire obsolète était souvent distribué.

C1 D'après l'uniforme de la Wasserschützpolizei; notez l'aigle sur la manche et l'écusson sur la casquette de style policier, et le ruban sur la manche de ce service. **C2** Uniforme d'officier de la Luftwaffe avec insigne des Beamten; le double fond rouge sur vert de la plaque d'épaule et la marque 'GFP' identifiaient cette arme particulière. **C3** A cette date-là, l'uniforme de la Kriegsmarine avait été adopté. La plaque de col est épinglée sur les revers.

D1 Hormis l'aigle argent sur la manche et le ruban de manche, l'uniforme est la tenue de campagne de base d'un officier de l'armée, la Waffenfarbe orange de cette arme. **D2** Seuls la plaque de col et le brassard marquent l'affectation temporaire de cet homme à la Feldgendarmerie. **D3** Les insignes de col et la tresse sur la manche indiquent le grade de sous-officier; la plaque de col de fabrication allemande porte des lettres hongroises.

E1 Nouveau-venu, il porte l'uniforme tropical courant; l'aigle sur la manche et la plaque de col (celle-ci étant rare parmi les officiers) ne sont pas montrés, et l'arme du service n'est indiquée que par le Waffenfarbe et le ruban sur la manche. **E2** Un uniforme montrant des signes d'usure à la longue dans les rudes conditions du désert. Notez la version tropicale des pattes d'épaule de grade, le ton brun-rouille remplaçant la tresse d'argent. **E3** Une variation des combinaisons fort discutées des uniformes italiens et allemands et insignes portés par le personnel SS italien avec une copie italienne de la plaque de col.

F1 Les insignes de col sont sur le fond blanc de cette division; seul le fond de la patte d'épaule indique l'arme de la police en campagne. Cet officier de la ligne de front, avec décorations de combat, porte des pantalons et bottes ordinaires de soldat. **F2** La plaque de col militaire est la seule indication que ce sous-officier parachutiste sert dans la Feldgendarmerie. **F3** Des uniformes gris campagne furent parfois distribués lorsque le nombre des membres de la division a été doublé à la fin de l'année 1944. Les insignes de la Luftwaffe sont exposés ici sur des vêtements gris; notez le ruban de manche de la division; ruban de manche de la Feldgendarmerie militaire porté par d'anciens policiers de carrière dans l'unité de police de la Division; et la plaque de col de la Luftwaffe.

G1 Il porte ici l'uniforme M1943 plus simple avec le Waffenfarbe distinctif orange; notez les rubans sur la manche ni le ruban de manche de la Feldgendarmerie. **G2** A cette date on ne porte plus l'aigle sur la manche ni le ruban de manche; l'uniforme de 1943 est beaucoup plus simple et de qualité bien inférieure par rapport aux précédents. **G3** Ce sous-officier tente de conserver son élégance malgré la très basse qualité de l'uniforme de 1944. L'aigle et le ruban sur la manche ont été abandonnés par décret officiel.

H1 Lancé dans l'action avec un Kampfgruppe, il a déjà des succès à son acquis avec la Panzerfaust. Seuls le liseré et la plaque de col sont d'une arme d'origine. **H2** Un mélange suffisamment courant d'articles anciens et neufs, portés par un sous-officier des redoutés 'chasseurs de tête' dans les dernières batailles. C'est un fantassin expérimenté et il porte le Waffenfarbe blanc. La plaque de col porte la légende 'Feldjägerkorps', le brassard rouge 'Oberkommando der Wehrmacht/Feldjäger'. Il porte le fusil SG44. **H3** En mission pour les alliés après la fin de la guerre, ce policier de la circulation porte toujours son uniforme (certains insignes ayant été retirés) et conserve un pistolet. Les pantalons sont dans une étoffe de camouflage italienne.

Farbtafeln

A1 Dieser Unteroffizier trägt die Ziviluniform der Gendarmerie mit Rangabzeichen der Armee und Brustadier. Zu beachten sind die Grüntöne der Polizeiuniform und das braune Innenfutter. **A2** Die Uniform eines Armee-Offiziers mit den Insignien im Stil des Heeresbeamten. Das Stoffband am Unterarm existierte bereits, aber deren Ausgabe und wann es getragen wurde sind nicht bekannt. **A3** Auffallend ist die Mischung aus Krageninsignien, dem Stil der Armee entsprechen und sich aus der polizeigrünen Waffenfarbe, dem SS-Adler und Schulterbzeichen zusammensetzte.

B1 Die Feldgendarmerie-Insignien—orangene Waffenfarbe, der bei der Polizei übliche Adler auf dem Ärmel, Stoffband um Unterarm und Kragenspiegel—wurden ab 1940 eingeführt. **B2** SS-Kragen, Schulterstreifen und Insignien an den Ärmeln der Armee-Uniform mit derselben orangefarbigen Paspel, Stoffband am Unterarm und Kragenspiegel wie in der Feldgendarmerie der Armee. Die Feldmütze der Armee hat nur die Kokarde, die mit dem Totenkopfabzeichen der SS getragen wurde. **B3** Die anfänglichen Uniformen beibehalten die Polizeifarben und das Schnittmuster bei; in diesem Beispiel mit der grünen Paspel der Schutzpolizei, die an den Manschetten, vorn auf der Uniformjacke, den Kragen- und Schulterabzeichen zu erkennen ist. Letztere wurden in der braunen und silbernen Polizeifarbe gehalten. Zu bemerken ist die einmalige Paspel an der Polizeikappe. Veraltete Armee-Ausrüstung wurde oft ausgegeben.

C1 Diese Uniform beruht auf der der Wasserschutzpolizei. Auffallend ist der Adler am Ärmel und wie bei der Polizei, die Kappeninsignien und das Stoffband am Unterarm in diesem Dienstbereich. **C2** Die Uniform eines Luftwaffe-Ozze-Offiziers mit Beamteninsignien. Der doppelte, rote und grüne Hintergrund des Schulterabzeichens und die Abkürzung 'GFP' war die Erkennungszeichen einer bestimmten Einheit. **C3** Zu diesem Zeitpunkt wurde die Kriegsmarine-Uniform bereits benutzt. Der Kragenspiegel wurde am River mit Nadeln befestigt.

D1 Ausser dem silberenen Adler am Ärmel und dem Stoffband am Unterarm, ist diese Uniform mit der orangenen Waffenfarbe die übliche Bekleidung eines Armee-Offiziers im Feld. **D2** Nur der Kragenspiegel und die Armbinde weisen darauf hin, dass dieser Mann nur verübergehend der Feldgendarmerie zugeteilt wurde. **D3** Die Krageninsignien und die Manschettententressen weisen auf den Rang des Unteroffiziers hin. Der in Deutschland gefertigte Kragenspiegel birgt einen ungarischen Schriftzug.

E1 Dieser Neuankömmling trägt die standardmässige Tropenuniform. Der Adler auf dem Ärmell und Kragenspiegel—bei der Offiziersuniform wenig verwendet—sind nicht zu sehen. Die Abteilung wird nur durch die Waffenfarbe und dem Stoffband am Unterarm ersichtlich. **E2** Diese Uniform wurde lange in der Wüste getragen. An der Tropenversion ist auffallend, dass die Schulterrangabzeichen anstelle der silbernen eine rostbraune Tresse hatten. **E3** Eine Variation der vieldiskutierten Kombinationen der italienischen und deutschen Uniformen und Insignien, die von der italienischen SS mit einer italienischen Kopie des Kragenspiegels getragen wurde.

F1 Die Krageninsignien haben für diesen Divisioinen einen weissen Hintergrund. Nur der Hintergrund der Schulterstreifen weist auf die Feldpolizeiabteilung hin. Dieser Frontoffizier mit den Kampfauszeichnungen trägt die herkömmlichen Soldatenhosen und Stiefel. **F2** Der Armeekragenspiegel weist nur darauf hin, dass dieser Unteroffizier der Fallschmirmspringer bei der Feldgendarmerie eingesetzt wird. **F3** Die feldgrauen Uniformen wurden manchmal ausgegeben, als sich die Divisionsgrösse Ende 1944 verdoppelte. Die Insignien der Luftwaffe sind hier auf der Armee-Uniform zu sehen. Zu bemerken ist das Stoffband am Unterarm dieser Division. Das Stoffband am Unterarm von der Armee-Feldgendarmerie wurde von ehemaligen Berufspolizisten der Divisionspolizei-Einheit zusammen mit dem Luftwaffe-Kragenspiegel getragen.

G1 Die einfachere M1943 Uniform wurde mit den auffallenden orangenen Waffenfarben getragen. Die Stoffbänder am Unterarm, die bei der Division und der SS-Feldgendarmerie benutzt wurden, sind hier zu sehen. **G2** Wader der Adler auf dem Ärmell noch das Stoffband wurde benutzt. Die Uniform aus dem Jahre 1943 ist wesentlich einfacher gestaltet und von niederer Qualität. **G3** Dieser Unteroffozier versucht mit seiner M1944 Uniform, die von schlechter Qualität zeugte, einen guten Eindruck zu hinterlassen. Gemäss offizieller Anweisung wurde der Adler am Ärmel und das Stoffband weggelassen.

H1 Er hat bereits bei der Panzerfaust Erfolge erzielt und befindet sich im Einsatz bei der Kampfgruppe. Nur die Paspel und der Kragenspiegel lassen seinen ursprünglichen Dienstbereich erkennen. **H2** Eine häufig anzutreffende Mischung aus altem und neuem Zubehör, das von diesem Unteroffizier, der gefürchteten 'Kopfjäger' während der letzten Kampfhandlungen getragen wurde. Er ist ein erfahrener Infanteriesoldat und trägt die weisse Waffenfarbe. Der Kragenspiegel birgt den Schriftzug 'Feldjägerkorps' und die rote Armbinde 'Oberkommando der Wehrmathc/Feldjäger'. Er ist mit einer SG44 bewaffnet. **H3** Nach Kriegsende unter dem Kommando der Alliierten, trägt dieser Verkehrspolizist immer noch die Uniform—einige Insignien wurden entfernt—und er behielt seine Pistole. Die Hosen sind aus italienischem Tarnmaterial hergestellt.